# Exploring Po[etry]

Compiled by John Foster

## Contents

Today I'm an explorer    *Richard James*    2
I'd like to be an astronaut    *Tony Bradman*    4
The cave    *Tony Mitton*    7
It's snowing    *Richard James*    10
Explorers    *John Foster*    12
In our attic    *Clive Webster*    16

**Acknowledgements**

The Editor and Publisher wish to thank the following who have kindly given permission for the use of copyright material:

Tony Bradman for 'I'd like to be an astronaut' © 1989 Tony Bradman; John Foster for 'Explorers' © 1996 John Foster; Richard James for 'It's snowing' and 'Today I'm an explorer' both © 1996 Richard James; Tony Mitton for 'The cave' © 1996 Tony Mitton; Clive Webster for 'In our attic' © 1996 Clive Webster.

# Today I'm an explorer

Today I'm an explorer.
I'm crawling on my knees.
The jungle's full of birds and bugs
And butterflies and bees.

I'm tracking jungle tigers.
I'm jumping jungle streams.
And when tonight I'm tucked up tight,
I'll dream my jungle dreams.

*Richard James*

# I'd like to be an astronaut

I'd like to be an astronaut
Zooming through the stars.
I'd visit lots of planets
Like Jupiter and Mars.

I'd like to roam the spaceways
Where no one's ever been,
Where planets orbit double suns
And where the skies are green.

I'd walk in alien jungles
On beaches wild and free,
And where the only footprints
Are those made by me.

I'd see the strangest deserts,
And maybe in the sands
I'd find a ruined city
Raised by alien hands.

I'd find a thousand treasures,
And then perhaps one day,
I'd meet a fellow traveller
In the Milky Way.

An alien from a planet
In a distant galaxy,
Roaming through the spaceways —
Just like me.

*Tony Bradman*

**The cave**

Can you be daring?
Can you be brave?
Will you come down
to explore the cave?

We'll put on our boots
and carefully tramp
down through the darkness,
all slimy and damp.

They say there's a chest
a hundred years old.
It's spilling over
with jewels and gold.

The pirates left it
and never returned.
Their ship caught fire
and the map got burned.

So I'll take the torch
and you take the sack.
Let's go down there
and bring some back.

But hush! There's a dragon
who just might waken,
if he hears any of it
being taken.

*Tony Mitton*

## It's snowing

It's snowing.
I'm going
To find my sleigh.
It's snowing.
I'm going
To the Pole today.
It's snowing.
I'm going
Where the blizzard howls,
Where the ice-cap creaks,
Where the white bear growls,
Where the glaciers gleam,
Where the penguins play.
It's snowing.
I'm going
To the Pole today.

Richard James

11

## Explorers

Our topic is Explorers.
I've been reading in my book
About the places where they went
And all the risks they took.

I've read about Columbus
And his brave Spanish crew
And how they reached America
In fourteen ninety-two.

I've read about Captain Scott
And how he bravely tried
To be the first to reach the Pole,
How he was trapped and died.

I've read of Mary Kingsley,
Of the jungles she walked through
And the rivers full of crocodiles
Where she paddled her canoe.

I've read of Marco Polo,
How he crossed the desert sands
And brought back silk and spices
From far-off eastern lands.

*John Foster*

## In our attic

I went up in our attic,
Climbing every creaking stair,
And looked for hidden treasure
That I knew was waiting there.

But then I started screaming.
It echoed through the house.
Instead of finding golden coins
I found a little mouse.

*Clive Webster*